At Work with John's Gospel

A spirituality for life's
fruitfulness in all our labours
Five Bible studies

Edited by John Bottomley

COVENTRY
PRESS

Published in Australia by
Coventry Press
33 Scoresby Road
Bayswater Vic. 3153
Australia

ISBN 978 0 648145 75 2

Cataloguing-in-Publication entry is available from the National Library of Australia
http:/catalogue.nla.gov.au/.

Text design by Filmshot Graphics (FSG)
Cover design by Ian James – www.jgd.com.au

Printed in Australia

CONTENTS

PREFACE

For the most part, Australians have embraced the ideology of work that measures personal worth by a person's achievements at work, but which then blames victims when they suffer harm. Too often we turn a blind eye to the harm caused by a market economy that values personal worth only in terms of paid work, and which celebrates greed and fosters injustice.

And the extent of work-related harm is considerable. We have known about the debilitating impact of unemployment for decades. At times, the stream of new research findings on work-related harm can feel overwhelming. Currently, work in 21st century Australia has been linked with heart disease, mental illness, diabetes, numerous cancers, traumatic incident deaths, injury, disability and poverty. Housework and voluntary work remain low status in our market economy. Yet such is the strength of the current beliefs about the virtue of hard work that the plight of victims is most often attributed to their bad luck or human error.

When our culture explains that injustice at work is usually the victim's fault, there is little reason to look for other causes. The major political parties contribute to the invisibility of work harm and its causes by their faith in the market economy to provide for human happiness and wellbeing. They assume economic growth has ultimate priority for social development, and the narrow focus of their economic debates ensures the 'almighty dollar' is central to human flourishing. *The* meaning of work is rarely at stake, and the belief that *God's intention* for our created order is crucial for economic, social and environmental practice is an irrelevance.

Sadly, Australian churches too often fail to equip their members to see beyond the prevailing beliefs that sustain this ideology about Australian working life. Our churches have largely accepted the prevailing belief that the worlds of work and faith should be kept separate: faith is a private matter for the family and personal life, while work especially is governed by the public realities of science, technology, politics and economics. The beliefs that govern church and nation tend to render work in the home invisible, and minimise the value of such labours of love.

But the pain of work-related harm does not conform to these ideological boundaries. Every congregation has members, or members' children (and grandchildren) who are suffering a work injury, or have been retrenched, are suffering a mental illness due to bullying, or sexual violence, or social isolation, or have tasted poverty due to under-payment, breach of contract, unemployment or corrupt behaviour. This pain and the associated cries of work-related injustice today constitute an unparalleled pastoral challenge.

John's gospel is uniquely placed in the New Testament scriptures to speak pastorally and with prophetic integrity to this very circumstance. The gospel addresses a community of followers of Jesus who have endured harm by being forced out of the Jewish synagogue. Their claim that Jesus is both messiah and Lord has upset the Jewish religious leaders' accommodation with the Roman Empire. John's gospel that Jesus Christ will free God's people from their slavery to imperial power is a direct challenge to the Judean leadership. And the claim that Jesus is Lord is a fundamental challenge to the lordship and god-status of the Roman Emperor.

Being a follower of Jesus is dangerous for the Johannine community. So John's identification of the death-dealing powers that face Jesus and his community holds a grim realism. While John focuses on welcoming all who believe in Jesus, his gospel also fearlessly exposes what is hidden by the forces of darkness. John maintains the tension between those who follow Christ and his work of liberation for the world, and the need to exclude those who are false shepherds, brigands and thieves.

In these five studies, all of this is in the background. Part of John's genius is to enter the depth of the faith challenges facing his church by his use of personal stories. In these stories Jesus meets with one person, and their conversation brings to the surface the many levels of injustice and exclusion that serve the needs of those who benefit from their accommodation with the religious and imperial powers. The personal nature of the stories also invited John's community, and now us, to identify with the main character Jesus has interacted with, so that by entering into the story we may see how God is present in the gospel story and our own story.

The studies are also an invitation to connect with other Christian study groups seeking to more faithfully follow Jesus at work.   At Creative Ministries Network Congregation, we believe that following Christ's mission for the Australian church necessarily engages us in a mission to work. We have established this mission at the heart of our congregation. Now we are seeking to build an ecumenical network of individuals, study groups and prayerful support with whom to share our vision. We seek to connect with people who will join with us as followers of Christ's mission to engage a spirituality of healing, justice and reconciliation in work and life.

You can partner with the mission to work through our website: www.creative.unitingchurch.org.au

John Bottomley

Coordinator

Mission to Work Project

with Michael Bastin, Steve Crump, and Keir Saltmarsh

NOTES FOR LEADERS

These studies are designed so that leadership may be shared within the study group. The leader for each study should read over the study well before the session. Some people may not be used to the generous amount of time for silent reflection and meditation given in this study. Encourage them to develop a patient and open attitude to this time of listening for God's voice.

Each person in the study group needs to have their own copy of *At Work with John's Gospel*. Participants will also need their own Bible, a pen, and paper to write on.

In Study Two, you will need a white-board and marker, or butcher's paper and texta.

Each study concludes with a simple ritual, using a symbolic object. Before the study begins, you will need to prepare the object to be used, and have a table that can be easily set up to provide a focus on which to place the object for the closing ritual.

Study one:	A glass of wine.
Study two:	A central candle.
	A fire-place, or container into which burning paper may be safely placed.
Study three:	A jug of ice water and a glass for each member of the group.
Study four:	A small bowl of vegetable oil, which has had several drops of perfume added.
Study five:	A central candle, and a smaller candle for each participant.
	A tray or bowl filled with sand to 2 cm depth (approx.).

INTRODUCTION

A primary identity-forming practice of the modern world is human work, and specifically, paid work. This study therefore comes to you as a counter-cultural experience, because it invites you to journey with Christ through John's gospel to the heart of God (John 1:18), so that your life and identity may be re-formed and renewed in Christ's 'grace and truth' (1:17). This can be an intimate journey as your life becomes enriched by your relationship with him.

The gospel is likely to have been written near the end of the first century C.E. There had been a period of relative peace in Jerusalem under Roman rule in the 50s due to an agreement with the Emperor on certain freedoms for the Judeans, but when the young Emperor Nero breached the agreement, it sparked a Judean revolt against the local authorities that precipitated the wrath of Roman imperial might against the minority Judeans. Their Jerusalem Temple was destroyed in 67 C.E., Galilean towns and villages were systematically destroyed, and thousands of civilians were killed. 'The oppressive presence of the Tenth Legion in the rubble of Jerusalem and in its outlying garrisons throughout Judea; the expropriation of significant tracts of agricultural land by the imperial authorities; and the loss of central leadership with the disappearance of the Jerusalem community of the movement left a spiritual vacuum for the disheartened follower of Jesus in Judea.'[1] John's gospel may best represent a direct literary response to this traumatic political circumstance, offering encouragement to the widely scattered and wounded community of Jews who believed Jesus was the promised messiah of Israel. John's gospel is good news for those traumatised and harmed by the accommodation of religious leadership to the prevailing political and economic order.

In John's gospel, it is Christ's call to his followers to have life in him that enables them to trust in God's sovereign power over the 'formless void and darkness' revealed in creation. For John, this darkness was represented by the violent power of imperial Rome, and for too

[1]R. Horsley and N. Silberman, *The Message and the Kingdom: how Jesus and Paul ignited a revolution and transformed the ancient world.* Fortress Press, Minneapolis, 2002, p. 218.

many today, is represented by the rapacious violence of a globalised economic system that causes harm in their everyday struggles in every sphere of work.

Our intention is to enter more deeply into the spiritual issues that lie at the heart of our formation in justice and human wholeness through our relationship with Christ and/or the culture of work, paid or unpaid. The study series invites you to deepen your awareness of how your life has been formed by your work, especially by your paid work. Work in its broadest sense is a sharing in God's creative activity. So work includes paid work, work in the home, and voluntary work.

You will be invited to meditate upon the Bible passage, and on your own experience at work and in life. This time is an invitation to silence, that in the silence, you may know God. You are invited to listen to the voice of God in your heart. This use of silent meditation is derived from 16th century Ignatian spiritual disciplines of contemplative prayer. This ancient wisdom creates a contemporary space to listen beneath the noise and busyness of our work, which too often shuts out silence and makes it difficult to discern God's presence.

In this series, the silence of the meditation times is offered to you as a gift. But don't be anxious if there are times when the silence seems unproductive. You are involved in a journey into the mystery of God's love, and what happens cannot be measured by the standards of the workplace. Be patient with yourself. Trust that you may hear God in the stillness.

After each meditation, the reflective process invites each person to share as much or as little of their reflection as you wish. Each member of the group is requested to listen respectfully and non-judgmentally to your group members' contributions. Once every person has shared, there may be a further round of sharing for anyone who has been inspired to offer more of their original reflection than they had at first. This time is not a time for discussion, but for deep listening and valuing the meditative reflections of others.

There are also times for discussion. Our congregation's experience in faith-sharing is to focus on acknowledging shared insights, and then to be open to individual differences. Allow yourself to be surprised by what others have experienced of Christ's presence or absence in their life and work!

Each study concludes with a simple shared ritual.

STUDY ONE

Transforming work

The leader reads.

John's gospel begins with Jesus' sign at Cana of God's transforming power.   Those who read John's gospel are left in no doubt from the very beginning of the narrative that John's whole literary undertaking is written so that his community might see in Jesus the glory of God as a transforming power.   Jesus has been sent as Israel's messiah to reveal God's liberating and life-giving presence in their troubled and violent world.

In this study:

- John's gospel quickly brings into view Jesus' humanity and compassion.

- John reveals that God's entire plan in sending Jesus is to transform our public humiliations and failures into life in its fullness.

- We learn that God enacts judgment on idolatrous powers in Christ's cleaning out a corrupted religious institution.

- We will see John's realism about the world's violence, and his trust that in Jesus we are seeing God's transforming power overcoming sin, evil and death.

The wedding host

A member of the group reads John 2:1-4.

Then one of the group members reads the following information.

Jesus and his disciples have been invited to a wedding in Cana, and the wine has run out. For the wedding host to run out of wine at such an important public event would have threatened a serious loss of family honour.   At first, Jesus shows no interest in the wedding host's humiliation.

Take at least five minutes for the following meditations.

Imagine you are Jesus' mother, and a guest at the wedding. How do you feel when you notice your neighbour and your host has run out of wine completely? You know your community will judge the situation as a shameful failure by the hosts.

Now become aware of times you have felt anxious or concerned that your work and life is about to fall apart. Notice you often feel empty within yourself when trouble looms. How does it feel if you experience emptiness with your work? Sit with this feeling. Be aware of your desire, your longing. As you listen to your own deepest desires, will you speak to Jesus about how you feel?

Share together your meditation on your longing for fullness in your work and how you feel about making your needs known to Jesus.

An emptiness transformed

A member of the group reads John 2:5-12.

Then one of the group members reads the following information.

The servants obey Jesus' instruction to fill water jars and miraculously draw off the best wine of the feast. John wants us to see that this friend of the family is utterly to be trusted, even when the command his mother gives to the servants makes no rational sense. This Jesus is the Christ, the messiah of Israel, whose actions save the wedding host from community humiliation and shame. John also indicates that the event has deeper significance. It is the very first sign in John of God's plan to send Jesus into our world to transform our public humiliations and failures into the glorious reality of life in its fullness.

Take at least five minutes for the following meditations.

Imagine you are the bridegroom. How do you feel being complimented on keeping the best wine until last? Like the disciples, you discern God's hand in Jesus' gift of kindness that has saved you from public humiliation. What is your attitude towards Jesus?

Now hear Jesus' desire to fill any emptiness in your work and life. What is your deepest longing, your real need for fullness or wholeness in your working life? Imagine the rich and fruitful flavour of your working life as it comes to fullness. What is your awareness of Jesus' longing for your relationship with him today?

Share together your meditation on your longing to be transformed for fullness in your work. Share how you experienced Jesus' presence (or absence) in this meditation.

A corrupted icon emptied

A member of the group reads John 2:13-25.

Then two or three of the group members each reads a paragraph from the following information.

Jesus drives the moneychangers from the Jerusalem Temple, while accusing them of turning the Temple into a marketplace. In contrast to the other gospels, John places the cleansing of the Temple at the very beginning of Jesus' ministry. But in common with them he places it within the context of the Passover Feast. Wright says, 'there is no doubt what John thinks it all means. It is Passover time; he has already told us that Jesus is God's Passover lamb (1:29) and now he goes to Jerusalem at the time when liberation, freedom, rescue from slavery was being celebrated. Somehow, John wants us to understand, that what Jesus did in the Temple is a hint at the new meaning he is giving to Passover'.[2]

Here, John's gospel further reveals its political character. The (Passover) lamb that takes away the sin of the world is not primarily concerned (as western theologies have for too long insisted) with freeing individuals from their 'sins'. The Temple was the centre of Judaism's worship, politics and economics; and the place where Israel's God had promised to live amongst God's people. As the centre of Judaism's political economy, its system of taxation and tributes benefited the social elites, who maintained their status under the patronage of the Roman Emperor. So Jesus breaks open the silence cloaking the political accommodation with Rome that favours the religious leaders of Jerusalem. With his incendiary denunciation Jesus turned everything upside down. Jesus clearly regards the Temple as corrupt. Then in claiming the true Temple is embodied in him, Jesus says his death and resurrection will reveal the fullness of Passover liberation for his oppressed people.

---

[2]N. T. Wright, *John for Everyone. Part 1 Chapters 1-10.* London, SPCK, 2002, p. 26.

John points out that the destruction and rebuilding of the Temple in three days is to be understood as a reference to Jesus' death and resurrection. There is a double allusion here – the end of the old corrupt system is being dismantled as an act of God's judgment, and there is the formation of something new out of this old system. When Jesus' followers remember his words, they 'believed the scriptures and the word that Jesus had spoken'. That is, they trusted in him.

For John, trust in Christ means adherence or loyalty to the community of faith. It is not holding a merely private opinion, nor expressing one's belief in secret. A public confession of allegiance to Jesus as Israel's messiah is called for. Taking the risk of being a member of this new group is a total transformation that is expected from those people who have faith in Christ. But to take that step meant leaving one of the established groups, which had previously been a source of security in an often threatening environment. This is a thread that is woven into everything that will follow. That thread will also trace where John's gospel is going, and what those who believe in Christ may also anticipate.

Discuss whether there is anything here that is new in your understanding of how John's gospel speaks about the meaning of Jesus' death and resurrection: as the Passover lamb that delivers freedom for people from political and economic oppression, and the sacrificial lamb that liberates people from the sin and evil of corrupted idols.

After this discussion, take at least five minutes for the following meditations.

Meditate on Jesus' anger at the corruption of the Temple's purpose through the expansion of the marketplace into the Temple's space for prayer and worship. Become aware of the corrupted forces that Jesus has called out through his words and actions. Reflect on Jesus' passion for the true worship of his Father God, and what that may mean for him in coming days.

Now recall a time when the boundaries of your work were violated by the priority given to political and/or economic demands. How did you feel? What did you do with your feelings? How did you experience God in that situation, at that time? What do you yearn for in such situations?

Share your meditation one by one. When everyone has spoken, reflect on any common themes. What do you think is the connection between the two stories John recounts in chapter two in relation to God's strategy for transforming work and life's emptiness, and emptying work and life's corruption of the 'powers that be'?

Closing prayer

A glass of wine is placed on a central table.

Leader: Let us open our hearts and minds to every sign that Christ is present in our daily work and life. We confess that too often our labour leaves us with empty hearts and distracted minds.

People: *O God, forgive us.*

Leader: We confess we hide our empty hearts from Christ with hard work and busy lives. We have lived to work, making our labour the centre of our relationships. We have placed our devotion to the idols of money, technology and power at the heart of our identity.

People: *O God, forgive us.*

Leader: We confess we have put our faith in these idols to solve our human problems. Our living has become competitive, anxious, soul-less. We have turned our eyes from the pollution of the environment by the demands of our industry.

People: *O God, forgive us.*

Leader: We confess the blindness of our belief: that fitting in with those in power will secure for ourselves the good life. We have become numb to the truth, we cannot hear the pain of others, and we justify our illusions as God's blessing.

People: *O God, forgive us.*

Lead our hearts to worship you alone, that our work will serve you humbly in the liberation of all people captive to exploitative powers and burdened by the idolatry of sin and evil. Amen.

The leader raises the cup of wine, and it is passed from one person to the next with the words, 'May the fullness of life in Christ free you - body, heart and mind - for service in solidarity with one another, Christ's new community'.

The leader offers a blessing.

STUDY TWO

Freedom from work, freedom for work

The leader reads.

In the first study, we saw Jesus transform work and life's emptiness with God's fullness of life. Out of his fullness as God's beloved son, Jesus then recasts national expectations about how salvation will come to his people by emptying the Temple of its corrupting influences. The idolatry of money and power are turned upside down and they and their devotees are driven out of God's house.   When John tells us of Jesus' awareness that these same forces will cause Jesus' death, it is so that Jesus can testify to his trust in God's power to raise him from death.   The transformation of the Temple is for John, a sign of the transformation of death yet to come.   This mystery God's transforming power is revealed as the source of life's fullness. Jesus' freedom to live life to the fullest is a gift from God, with whom Jesus is intimately related.

In this study:

- We will meet Nicodemus who wants Jesus to give him this freedom; and we will recall our own desire for freedom in our working life.

- With Nicodemus, we will listen to Jesus teaching us about how we may receive this gift.

- We will also listen to how the freedom Jesus has relates to the values and structures of work today.

- Then we will rejoice in the price God paid for our freedom; and encounter what Christ's death means for our freedom at work.

Nicodemus

A member of the group reads John 3:1-2.

Then one of the group members reads the following information.

Nicodemus is a representative of intelligent, discerning, religious Judaism, a Pharisee, and he can see that Jesus' activity has God's blessing on it. Nicodemus would love to know more from Jesus. But Jesus has just caused trouble at the Temple (John 2:13-16), and the Temple is at the heart of Judaism. Good order there is central to the religious leaders such as Nicodemus maintaining their privileged position, which rests on them maintaining good relations with the Roman Empire. But Jesus has just driven out the money-changers, and overturned their tables, disrupting preparations for the great feast of Passover that is about to begin. There is more than a whiff of civil disobedience about Jesus' actions, which threatens the religious compromise with a pagan Empire. Perhaps Nicodemus thought it unwise to be seen in Jesus' presence, for Nicodemus approaches Jesus under cover of darkness.

Take at least five minutes for the following meditations.

Imagine what Nicodemus experiences as he seeks Jesus out - his longing and his fears. What is the deep longing in Nicodemus' heart? What is Nicodemus afraid of?

Now, meditate upon your deepest longing for your life at work - your work in the home, as a volunteer, and/or in paid employment. What do you desire? As you listen to your own deepest desires, what fears touch your heart?

Share together your meditation on your longing for your work and your fears.

Nicodemus and Jesus

A member of the group reads John 3:3-12.

Then one or more of the group members read the following information.

Jesus tells Nicodemus how he can embrace his deepest longing, how he can enter into God's community of relationships, the 'kingdom of God'. He must be born from 'above', which in the worldview of the day meant the realm where God dwells. In the status hierarchy of Roman society, Jesus invites Nicodemus to become a child of God. Such a birth status was the highest status imaginable, and overturned the status hierarchies of wealth and power inherited by birth in Roman society. But perhaps the darkness of night limits Nicodemus' ability to see in more ways than one.

Nicodemus stands in the physical world, and seems not to see more than the physical things that give him a privileged position in Jewish society, and give him privileges in Roman society not available to other Jews and non-Roman citizens. So perhaps with a mounting anxiety about what Jesus' words may mean for him, Nicodemus asks, 'how can a person be born again?' But the new birth Jesus is talking about is of a different order. Jesus is saying that God desires to make equal all who follow Jesus. And more than that, the equality they are born into confers the new status of children of God. As children of the heavenly realm of God, they are born into the highest status of all.

Nicodemus asks 'how', and Jesus responds by talking about birth, wind and Spirit. Nicodemus wants an answer, a method or a technique he can apply to achieve this renewed life. And Jesus responds with these mysterious, uncontrollable events in life - birth, wind, Spirit. Jesus says that these are what give life in the kingdom of God. Life is a gift, not something we can control by our piety or our power. Life's fullness is to be received as a powerful, uncontrollable and mysterious gift that allows a person to be born anew, to be renewed from top to bottom as equal persons sharing the high birth status of children of God.

Nicodemus is a teacher of Jewish law, and knows how to apply his own faith to his everyday life. He has learnt all his religion has to teach him about gaining fulfilment. Yet in meeting Jesus, Nicodemus feels in his heart that God has more that may fulfil his life. Until he met Jesus, Nicodemus believed his religion ordered his life with commands and instructions to be learnt and applied. So he thinks he can learn Jesus' new rules, and gain that extra fulfilment he feels he is lacking. But, in the context of how Nicodemus lived his faith up to that point, Jesus' words simply do not make sense to him.

Take at least five minutes for the following meditations.

Imagine what it is like for Nicodemus with his heart tugging in the direction of freedom and equality, and his mind holding tight to the dictates of good order and personal security. How does Nicodemus feel as his central beliefs about God, his identity and his society are called into question?

Now, recall when you have experienced that much (or some) of what you believed about work, God's goodness and our society was called into question. How did it feel when beliefs you had grown up with felt no longer as true for you as they once were? What did your inner conflict feel like?

Share together your meditation on when your experience of work brought you into conflict with your beliefs about God, work and society.

Jesus

A member of the group reads John 3:13-17.

Then one of the group members reads the following information.

Jesus reminds Nicodemus of a story in the Book of Numbers (21:4-9). The people of Israel had considered that their suffering from a plague of snakes was God's punishment for sin. But when Moses obeyed God's command to lift up a bronze serpent upon a pole, all who had snake bites recovered from the snake's poison if they looked upon the bronze serpent. In the same way, Jesus being lifted up on the cross will be a source of salvation for all who believe in his power to save people.

On the cross, the relationship between God the Father and God the Son is transformed. Because God the Father loves the world so much, God lets go of Jesus' life for the sake of the world's need for redemption. The Father does not control Jesus' life, or seek to protect Jesus from the sinful world that can no longer abide Jesus' presence in the world. And Jesus lets go of dependence upon the Father, and chooses the way his life must go, even though it means his death.

John's gospel here presents the saving mystery of Christ's death and resurrection. The Father accepts that God must be powerless in our world so that Jesus is free to experience the anguish and pain of the world's violence arising from its idolatry and sin. At the same time, Jesus' freedom to choose to endure the world's evil without divine protection reveals the depth of his humanity. In God's gift to Jesus of his freedom to live a fully human life in the world, and Jesus' free choice to enter fully into the world's violence and death, a new and powerful relationship of suffering love is born between Father and Son. This love becomes God's gift to our world. Here is the mystery of birth from 'above'. It is birth into life in God, life in the freedom of the love given between the Father and the Son, which, for John, is fully realised on the cross.

Discuss whether there is anything here that is new in your understanding of how John's gospel understands the relationship between the Son and the Father being fulfilled on the cross for the sake of the world.

After this discussion, take at least five minutes for the following meditations.

Meditate for a time on Jesus' awareness of God's love for him and the world. How does Jesus feel knowing God's love constrains God to powerlessness if he is to ensure Jesus' freedom in the world? Then become aware of how Jesus feels as he chooses to give up his life in obedience to his understanding that his Father God's commitment to human freedom means Jesus must face the anguish of crucifixion totally alone?

Now recall a time when you felt God was calling you to give up something in your working life that might cause you to suffer for the cause of justice, or human dignity, or the wellbeing of another. How did you feel? How did you experience God's presence at this time?

When you are ready, each person writes on a small piece of paper the thing that they gave up. After all have finished writing, share together your meditation on your experience of God's presence when giving up something in your working life for the cause of justice, or human dignity, or the wellbeing of another.

Closing prayer

Bring the room to darkness, and light a central candle.

Leader: We come to Jesus through the darkness as Nicodemus came to Jesus by night.

(Each person in turn may read one of the following prayers of thanksgiving.)

Thank you, Lord, for the security of the darkness in our lives, which hides our fears, and cloaks our anxiety.

Thank you, Lord, for the loneliness of our darkness, which draws us to stand within our fears and anxiety. Thank you, Lord, for the darkness of Christ's cross, that reveals our sorrow for our fears and anxiety.

Thank you, Lord, for the silence of our darkness, from which springs your word of healing grace, to bring new life and purpose from our fears and anxiety,

Leader: We come to Jesus now in the darkness, asking to be born anew in solidarity with Christ and his liberated and liberating community.

In turn, each member is invited to light from the central candle their piece of paper naming what they gave up for the sake of another, then to drop their burned up paper into a fire-proof container.

After all have completed this ritual.

Leader: We thank you, Christ our Liberator, that through your great love

People: you are at one with us in solidarity, so that all who are burdened by fear and powerlessness may be liberated to life in its wholeness. Amen.

STUDY THREE

Thirsting for life and truth in work relations

The leader reads the following information.

When we meet the Samaritan woman in this study, we will encounter our own prejudices, which close our eyes and ears to the gifts of food and water Jesus offers to nurture our spirits. With the Samaritan woman, we will discover how persistent is Jesus in breaking through our prejudices, and how slow we are to let go of the comfortable stereotypes that shape our participation in our work-a-day world. Then we will listen to Jesus teaching the disciples and the Samaritans, and taste the life-giving solidarity that Jesus' Word creates in our work relationships.

The Samaritan woman

A member of the group reads John 4:5-12.

Then one or more of the group members reads the following information.

Jesus' encounter with the Samaritan woman by Jacob's well is a meeting that takes place in an atmosphere of prejudice and arrogance. The Jews and Samaritans carried a long standing tension between them. The Jews considered the Samaritans reactionaries, and viewed them as unclean. Even for a Jew such as Jesus to talk with a Samaritan was an act of ritual uncleanness. The Samaritans, for their part, viewed the Jews as heretics who had betrayed God's covenant by adding other books to the first five books of the Bible.

It was also unethical for Jesus, as a good Jew, to be seen talking privately with a woman. So, their meeting takes place in an atmosphere that is ripe for conflict and misunderstanding. Not surprisingly then, the Samaritan woman first sees Jesus only as a Jew and someone to be rid of as quickly as possible (4:11-12).

The Samaritan woman cannot see who Jesus is because she is caught up in the prejudice and arrogance of traditional Samaritan-Jewish rivalry. It is her fear of 'Jews' that motivates her to push Jesus away. Fear throws up a barrier between them.

Take at least five minutes for the following meditations.

Imagine how the Samaritan woman feels as this anonymous 'Jew' demands a drink from her. Hear the disdain in her question. Sense the mockery in her words to the 'Jew'. What is she feeling in her heart as she establishes a clear boundary for her meeting with the 'Jew'?

Now recall when you have had similar feeling at your work? How did you feel about the other person(s) when these feeling arose? How did you feel about yourself when these feeling arose?

Share together your meditation on your feelings that have arisen when meeting a person whom you felt was different to yourself and/or those with whom you have been familiar in your work.

Jesus and the Samaritan woman

A member of the group reads John 4:13-30.

Then one or more of the group members reads the following information.

It is prejudice that attacks Jesus - a prejudice built up over life-times between Samaritans and Jews, a prejudice that is like a sleeping tiger, which, when scratched, springs to life. Yet Jesus meets the Samaritan woman's ridicule and arrogance with renewed honesty and openness. Suddenly, the one who asked for a drink is offering a drink (4:13-14).

The thirst Jesus is speaking of is not a physical thirst, but it is the thirst for God's righteousness, God's justice. The Samaritan woman knows something of this deep thirst for God's righteousness, and for the first time she replies to Jesus with an openness and directness that begins to reveal her deepest needs (4:15-19).

Once the Samaritan woman had opened her heart to Jesus, Jesus penetrated to the source of hidden pain in her life. There is no judgment by Jesus of this deep pain in her life. We do not know the circumstances of her five previous marriages, or of her current de-facto relationship. We do not know from Jesus whether her hidden pain is caused by divorce or the deaths of her previous husbands.

All we know is that as the Samaritan woman opened her heart to Jesus, then Jesus looked into the depths of her heart and saw her deep-felt anguish. Jesus heard in his own heart this woman cry for God's righteousness: for her life to be put right. When Jesus offered the Samaritan woman a spring of living water inside her that would well up to eternal life, to wholeness, she knew that this was what she thirsted for.

Jesus' judgment on the hidden suffering of the Samaritan woman is full of mercy and grace. This is God's righteousness and justice. The woman herself now sees Jesus with new eyes (4:20). From her initial fear, prejudice and arrogance, the woman has moved to meeting Jesus as another human being. Now she begins to see a greater depth in him that is living water for her tortured and anguished heart. The woman's new openness to Jesus leads her to be offered one final revelation (4:23-24).

The term 'spirit' describes God's activity. In this context, a better translation for 'spirit' might be 'life-giving'. God gives life because it is God's Spirit within us that animates us, which enlivens us. God's Spirit is God's 'breath', as the creation story in Genesis puts it. The final movement in this encounter is the invitation to worship in spirit and truth. It is the realisation by this woman that Jesus has given her God's precious gifts of life and truth to be the new centre of her life (4:25, 26, 29).

Take at least five minutes for the following meditations.

Meditate on the spiritual journey of the Samaritan woman. Imagine how she feels as the hostility and fear she felt on meeting the 'Jew' is transformed by Jesus' merciful acceptance of the deep hidden pain and suffering of her heart. Taste her bitter-sweet yearning for something more in her life. Then feel her heart open to the wonderful discovery of the spirit and truth that give depth to her life, and that draws her life into the creative activity of the Christ.

Now recall a time when your attitude to another person changed from fear or suspicion to a deeper acceptance of their humanity. Become aware of God's Spirit present with you in your process of transformation. How do you feel about the change that took place within you and within that relationship? What is your response to God?

Share together your meditation.

Then discuss what you have learned together about the 'life and truth' of God's Spirit when it is present in such situations. What has God's Spirit taught you about yourself and your relationship with Christ?

The Samaritans

Finally, a member of the group reads John 4:31-42.

Then one of the group members reads the following information.

By sharing her experience of Christ, the Samaritan woman has sown the seed of faith in the lives of others in her community. Then she and many other Samaritans stepped forward into a wonderfully renewed vision of life, as people made whole by God's righteousness and justice now alive in their hearts (4:39-42).

The witness of one woman opens the way for others who received her testimony to discover the fruitful spirit and truth of God in Christ. Her response to Jesus has enabled others to taste the food and drink of God's unconditional love by which Jesus nurtures his followers, building a new community.

Take at least five minutes for the following meditations.

Reflect with joy and thanks on the Samaritan woman's experience of personal liberation that opened the way for Christ's life-giving grace to renew her life and her community. Meditate on this miracle of faith.

Then reflect further on your relationships in this study. What are the stories that have spoken to your heart and brought you a sense of freedom and joy? And what is the effect of your shared faith for your work and your personal life?

Share together your meditation.

What movement do you discern within your study group as members of Christ's new community of righteousness and justice for work and life?

Closing prayer

A jug of ice water is placed on a table, with a glass for each member of the group.

Leader: Let us give thanks for the gift of water,
that brings growth to the earth
that cleans our bodies,
that refreshes our spirits,
that, through baptism,
raises us with Christ
from death to newness of life.

Response: *Lord Jesus, give me that living water.*

Leader: We are thirsty for righteousness,
for our waters are polluted,
our bodies have been broken,
our spirits have been crushed,
and the pain of our suffering remains
hidden deeply from our narrow vision.

Response: *Lord Jesus, give me that living water.*

Leader: Take this water,
and taste Christ's living water
that wells up to eternal life.
Drink, and know that from today
you live in spirit and in truth.

Response: *Lord Jesus, give me that living water.*

The leader pours a glass of water for each person from the jug, and invites them to drink. There is a time of silence.

Leader: When you drink the water that Christ gives, you are born into solidarity with all those who cry out from the agony of injustice and prejudice. Open your hearts to receive what you desire, the gift of righteousness and justice.

The prayer concludes with group members invited to share the blessing of Christ's Peace with each other. One or both may say, 'The peace of the Lord be with you'. A response may be, 'And also with you'.

STUDY FOUR

Solidarity and healing at work

The leader reads this introduction to the study.

At the end of Study Three, we affirmed the life-giving community and solidarity Jesus' Word creates in our work relationships, indeed, in all of life. Study Four explores in greater depth our need for solidarity with Christ in our work, and in our whole life. With the man born blind we encounter the solidarity Jesus offers that meets our deepest needs amongst the conflicting needs of our working lives - our need for acceptance, trust and solidarity.

The solidarity we discover with Jesus is strengthened again and again as our struggles for wholeness intensify. Through Jesus' solidarity with us, we can finally see what is of ultimate value in our life and work. Solidarity with Jesus leads us beyond ourselves and our struggles into worship of God. There, with the man born blind and now healed and restored to the fullness of life in Jesus' community, we can offer praise for how God is working for our good in all things.

A man blind from birth

A member of the group reads John 9:1-7.

Then one or more of the group members reads the following information.

In Jewish society in Jesus' day, a disability such as blindness could be attributed to sin. So the Pharisees avoid contact with the man born blind because they do not want to become ritually impure. The religious purity of the Jewish community gave it social cohesion and unity of purpose, and was the key to the Pharisees' ambitions to resist the Roman Emperor's military-backed idolatry and eventually be liberated from pagan oppression.

So too the disciples are keen to step back from the blind man's suffering. Their ploy is to escape into an abstract theological discussion about the cause of his blindness. Such is the power of the Pharisees to influence people's behaviour towards conformity with their religious convictions and social-political goals!

Jesus doesn't waste time on such diversions - he simply acts. He touched the blind man, putting a paste of spittle and dust on the man's eyes. Jesus stood alongside the man, and ministered to him in response to his need. And by Jesus' gracious love, the blind man was able to see.

Take at least five minutes to meditate on the following two situations.

First, imagine yourself as the man born blind. How do you feel living without sight? What is that like? What is it like to be constantly reminded that your blindness is either your fault or your parents' fault? Then someone touches your eyes, an act that is forbidden by the ritually pure Pharisees. How do you feel? How do you feel next when Jesus sends you to wash at the pool of Siloam? And then you can see! How do you feel about being able to see for the first time in your life?

And secondly, recall a time from your work or your life where you were suffering, and felt cut off from people through no fault of your own, and alone. How did you feel? What was it like to feel that you were being blamed for your situation, when you could not defend your reputation? Recall whether you received any support. Where did your support come from? How did you feel? Become aware of your deepest desire for new insight into your experience. Imagine your eyes being opened to new insight into yourself, and your situation. How do you feel with this new insight?

Share together your meditation.

The Pharisees and the man blind from birth

A member of the group reads John 9:8-34.

Then one or more of the group members reads the following information.

John's gospel makes it clear that Jesus' acts of compassion for others is in conflict with the religious leaders' view of God's intention for human flourishing. The religious leaders' concern for maintaining religious purity through good order is a political necessity if they are to protect their community from the influence of the pagan Romans. But all their efforts are being undermined by Jesus' public healing of the man blind from birth. Jesus had healed the blind man on the Sabbath - an offence against the Pharisees' view of God's commands for proper Sabbath observance. For them, Jesus' act of healing puts at risk the security of Jewish identity they worked so hard to maintain under Roman rule, an identity that could only be maintained by their ritual purity, which separated them from pagan defilement.

To uphold their belief, and manage the risk Jesus posed to their community, the Pharisees must discredit Jesus. So they begin to put pressure on the healed man to declare that Jesus is a sinner who has undermined Jewish law. Then the Pharisees put pressure on the healed man's parents. Like the disciples earlier, the parents are keen to avoid trouble with the Pharisees. But the healed man states the healing of his blindness could come only from God.

At this, the Pharisees explode, condemning the healed man as a sinner from birth, and casting him out of the community. What a high price he pays for his healing! Born blind, he has been an outcast all his life. And having been healed by Jesus, the man falls foul of those devoted to keeping social cohesion through strict religious order. Once again, he is cast out!

Take at least five minutes for the following meditations.

Imagine being the man recently healed of your blindness and now facing criticism from the powerful leaders of your community, even as those closest to you step away from you and abandon you to your fate with those in power. How do you feel? Where was the one who healed you when you experienced this abuse?

Recall a time from your work or non-work life where you believed yourself to be a person of worth, then you found yourself being criticised and attacked in a very personal and abusive way for matters that seemed without foundation. How did you feel? Where was Christ in your life at this time?

Share together your meditations.

Jesus and the healed man

A member of the group reads John 9:35-41.

Then one or more of the group members reads the following information.

It is at the very point where the conflict seems to be at its greatest that the real miracle occurs. At the height of the conflict that his healing had provoked, Jesus comes and stands beside the man again.

This time, the solidarity Jesus extends is at a far deeper level than any mere physical cure. Jesus offers the solidarity of communion with God, and announces judgment on the blindness of the Pharisees. The one who was judged to be born in sin is saved. He is made whole, not by receiving the gift of his physical sight, but by receiving the spiritual insight that in Jesus he has been renewed in relationship with God and God's people.

His response is no mere thanks. The man turns to Jesus, the Messiah of Israel, who has come to free Israel from slavery to sin and evil, and greets him with worship and praise. This act provides the healed man with a new experience of solidarity. It is the solidarity of open-hearted love, which unites him with his Lord and God, and which welcomes him into Jesus' new community of thanksgiving and joy.

Take at least five minutes for the following meditations.

Imagine you are the healed man. You open your heart in wonder and gratitude to Jesus as your solidarity with God's love fills your life and you enter a deep communion of grace-filled love. Then you hear Jesus' judgment against the religious leaders for their spiritual blindness. How do you feel? Taste the fullness of God's solidarity with you in unconditional love.

Now recall a time in your life or work when you felt God's presence in a powerful way that lifted your heart and strengthened your faith. Then be aware of a time when you were able to see clearly the spiritual blindness of those who abused their power for their own ends. How did you feel towards them? What is Christ saying to you about your healing and wholeness of life?

Share together your meditation.

Then the leader reads the following:

The world of work has usually talked about solidarity through the exercise of power and strength. But John leads us to see a new form of solidarity that is the gift of God's love uniting those who know their weakness and vulnerability, and who trust the strength of God's love for their healing and renewed community life. Discuss together 'How is God's deepest desire for communion with people being revealed in the work of your study group?'

Closing prayer

A small bowl of perfumed vegetable oil is placed on a central table.

Leader: Hear the voices of ill-health and injustice in our places of work.

Voice 1: *If I don't keep control, I may get hurt. I can't trust them not to take advantage of me.*

Voice 2: *Why do I so often feel I will be betrayed? Is it because I was abused as a child?*

Voice 3: *I try to fit in, but I usually feel worse when I do. It's like I am invisible.*

Voice 1: *I try to help whenever I can, but I'm tired of working 50 to 60 hours a week.*

Voice 2: *I hate the way they yell at me. My dad was always screaming at us kids.*

Voice 3: *I still remember crying for hours in the ladies toilets at work the first week after my mum died.*

Leader: Is any one among you suffering … or sick? Call for the elders of the church, and let them pray over you, anointing you with oil in the name of the Lord (James 5:13-14).

The leader anoints the person next to them with the perfumed oil by making the sign of the cross with the oil for healing on the person's forehead (or wrist), saying, 'Be healed of your suffering and the pain of injustice, in the name of Jesus Christ'.

Each anoints their neighbour in turn.

All stand and join hands in a circle.

Together: Christ is one with us in our suffering. We are one with Christ through his healing grace. We are joined in solidarity with Christ through the power of God's unconditional love. Amen.

STUDY FIVE

In the darkness of death, life

The leader reads the following introduction.

The darkness that from time to time surrounds our lives reaches its depths as we enter the darkness of death. This study brings us into the midst of the suffering and pain of death. We hear from his sister that Lazarus had died, and we go with Jesus to Lazarus' tomb.

This encounter encourages us to explore both how we respond to death in our place of work, as well as the 'deadness' we may experience in our work. Through this encounter, we receive again the truth we received in Study One – Jesus offers us freedom. Not even the barriers of death can contain or overcome Jesus' power to bestow the gift of freedom on our lives. We explore what this means for living with death when its shadow falls on our working life, and for being freed from our own 'deadness'.

Lazarus is dead!

A member of the group reads John 11:1-39.

Then one or more of the group members reads the following information.

John's account leaves us in no doubt that Lazarus is dead. The first message Jesus receives tells him Lazarus is ill, but by the time Jesus is ready to head for Judea, Lazarus has died. The disciples are unsure about this, thinking Lazarus is only resting, and could be healed (vv.1-16). From here, John piles up the evidence. Lazarus is surely dead!

- On arriving, Lazarus had been in the tomb for four days (v. 17).
- Martha confirms the fact (v. 21).
- Mary repeats Martha words (v. 32), and weeps with grief (v. 33).
- Jesus expresses his own grief (v. 35).

- The Jews' implied criticism of Jesus confirms Lazarus' death (v. 37).

- Jesus comes to the place of death - Lazarus' tomb (v. 38).

- Martha warns Jesus not to unseal the tomb because that will release the smell of death (v. 39).

Yes. Lazarus is dead. Perhaps it is important for John that those who read his gospel understand that Jesus was 'acquainted with grief' and knew the reality of death. Why is this important for John? The heart of John's gospel is that from the very moment of Christ's death, we are to see that God's love is stronger than death. So all of this encounter is John's prelude to the narrative of Christ's death and the power of God's suffering, forgiving, reconciling love that is revealed on the cross. John's resurrection accounts are then further testimony for this truth.

If John's gospel of Jesus' resurrection from the dead is to have meaning, Jesus' grasp of the reality of death is fundamental. To emphasise the importance of this, John not only builds the dramatic reality of Lazarus' death, he also draws our attention to a recent attempt by the Jerusalem religious establishment to kill Jesus, and the disciples' fear that going to be with Lazarus in Jerusalem is walking into a death trap (11:8). For John, the awful reality of death is soberly recounted, so that the power of God's life-giving love will be received by followers of the resurrected Jesus as the ultimate and trustworthy source of truth and life.

Take at least five minutes for the following meditations.

Imagine you are Jesus. Be aware of the disciples' fear that your death is immanent. How do you feel? You use 'sleeping' as a euphemism for death, but put it aside to speak plainly of death. Then you enter into the reality of Lazarus' death: its physical decay, its heart-wrenching grief, its finger pointing blame-shifting and then the emptiness of his absence. Taste your tears in the face of death's reality. How does the reality of death feel?

Now recall any experience of death at your work, and/or 'deadness' in your work or in other parts of your life. Be aware of any times when you used euphemisms to speak of death, and other times when the reality of death and life/work's 'deadness' could not be side-stepped. Recall how the power of death affected your life. How did you feel?

Share together your meditations.

Then discuss with the members of your study group what you have felt discussing your meditation on death and deadness at work or in life.

Lazarus is alive!

A member of the group reads John 11:40-44.

Then one or more of the group members read the following information.

Even though he sheds tears at Lazarus' death, Jesus is not daunted by the barriers of death. With the Samaritan woman, Jesus crossed the barriers of racial, religious and gender divisions. With the man born blind, Jesus crossed the barriers of illness and injustice. In both cases, Jesus demonstrated the miraculous power of God's love to renew life, to overcome the barriers that left people trapped in their isolation and hopelessness. Now, Jesus addresses the barriers of death itself. Here is God's messiah anointed for the purpose of Israel's liberation, not only from foreign powers, but now also for liberation from sin, idolatry and their death-dealing consequences. How will the power of God's mercy in the hands of Jesus address the four-days dead Lazarus? This is the final barrier Jesus must overcome in John's gospel before he encounters his own death and places his life and death in God's hands.

Share together your meditation.

Imagine now that you are Lazarus. You are cold, lifeless, and dead to the world in the dark silence of your tomb. You are dead, yet you hear a voice, calling you to life. Taste the depth of this miracle. How do you feel as the power of God's unconditional love speaks to all that is dead in you, calling you to life? Be aware of what is happening to the darkness, the emptiness, the deadness of your tomb. Feel all the things that have bound you being loosened. How do you feel as the life-giving spirit of new possibilities surges through you?

Recall the experience of death or 'deadness' in your work or life, and listen again. Listen for Christ's voice speaking to your heart and calling you from your deadness to life.   Become aware of Christ's love touching a place you have had barricaded, and pay attention to its power enlivening your heart.   What do you desire to be freed from? Reflect on what you are being called out to.

Share together your meditation.

Then discuss: How has this study series formed your relationship with Christ and your identity at work and in life?

Closing prayer

A candle is placed on a central table. Smaller candles are also provided, one for each person. A tray or bowl filled with sand to 2 cm. depth (approx.) is also placed on the table.

The main candle is lit.

Leader: The light shines in the darkness, and the darkness has not overcome it.

Portion of Psalm 116 is read with two groups reading alternate verses.

I love the Lord because he has heard my voice in supplication,

Because he has inclined his ear to me the day I called.

The cords of death encompassed me; I found trouble and sorrow.

But I called on the name of the Lord, 'O Lord, deliver me'.

Gracious is the Lord and just; our God is merciful.

The   Lord   guards   the   little   ones when I am brought low he delivers me.

Return, O my spirit, to your rest, for the Lord has been good to you.

For he has set me free from death, my eyes from tears, my feet from stumbling.

I shall walk before the Lord in the land of the living.

Each person is invited to light their candle from the main candle as a prayer asking for Christ's love to shine in the dark corners of your heart and soul. The lit candle is stood in the sand-tray.

Leader: Lord Jesus Christ, through your passion, lead us from death to life.   Unbind our grief and free us from all that barricades our broken hearts from receiving your light and love. Unite us in love with all who yearn for justice and mercy in their working lives. Fill the whole of our lives with your eternal love so that we may live in freedom as a life-giving people. Amen.

The prayer concludes with group members invited to share the blessing of Christ's Peace with each other. One or both may say, 'The peace of the Lord be with you'. A response may be, 'And also with you'.

MISSION TO WORK

The Mission to Work Project is an initiative of our Creative Ministries Network Congregation of the Uniting Church in Australia. We understand that the fundamentals that have formed our workplaces are the globalised and secular forces of a capitalist, free market economy. We also believe the Church is catholic, Spirit-filled, and gifted with Christ's call to justice and peace. So for those who recognise we work and live in the space where these two realities meet in our everyday lives, there is a need to connect and build networks with others who share our faith and social reality.

At Work with John's Gospel is a Bible study that is an important part of our ministry of nurturing congregations and their members for a collective and personal mission to work. We believe Bible study, prayer and worship are foundational for the re-formation of Christians for this too-long neglected mission.

We invite congregations and study groups to register their participation in studying *At Work with John's Gospel* on our website. Our website has further background reading on work and faith, and provides opportunities for feedback and comment on the study and the matters about which your group is concerned. We offer liturgical resources and sermons on work themes.

Our website will be a focus for shared information about the mission to work. On our website you will be able to keep in touch with other initiatives for an international and ecumenical mission to work. We plan to develop a theology of work, along with a project on responding to work-related trauma and a study of the spirituality of death, which links our understanding of death to 'the wages of sin', that is, the bitter fruit of work-related harm and injustice.

We welcome your interest, your prayers and comments as the mission unfolds. We believe it is vital to the coming of God's reign of healing, justice and reconciliation on earth.

Our web address: www.creative.unitingchurch.org.au